On an Island Surrounded by Water

On an Island Surrounded by Water

Christopher McMaster

Author

Southern Skies Publications

www.christophermcmaster.com

www.southernskiespublications.com

First Printing, 2021

For Rory, welcome to Earth! There's a wooden box with a lot of this stuff in that you (and any brothers, sisters or cousins) can have when I'm not around anymore

Contents

A Bit of an Explanation in the Form of an Introduction

Twenty years ago, I left the British Isles. I was happy to do so at the time, always the foreigner, always the one with an accent. But returning to the US I was again the one speaking funny or different. Words and phrases and pronunciations inhabited my tongue, moved right in without my even noticing. Now I always get the question, 'Where are you from?' no matter where I am. My answer is usually, 'California', the place where I was born. I notice that most of the time I don't even mention Britain. That is a disservice. The place helped shape me more than I can know. I spent most of my formative years on those islands. It is where I learned how to be a grown up.

I spent a year in London during my undergraduate studies. I fell in love, brought back my lady, and once my degree was in hand, returned to the UK with a baby in tow. To be honest, it took a few years to settle in. I remember looking over a lush green field about three years in and thinking something like, "It ain't so bad. Pretty even." Lonely, painful and hard sometimes, most definitely. Often, I felt like the fast forward button was pressed on my life experience, and I was helpless with the controls. There was no pause button.

Saying that, my experience there was also colourful and rich and life affirming. Life changing. I made a lot of mistakes, but always had a wiser me on my shoulder telling me to pay attention and learn, because if I didn't grasp the lesson being taught, it would be retaught even more painfully, until I grew. I am grateful for that.

But there was always an urge to return, to go 'home', and after nearly fourteen years I did. This little book is remembrance from that time, twenty years ago. Some vignettes ('what can be written on a vine leaf'), some poetry, a few stories.

Before I left, while on a trip to Venice, I found a handmade notebook—leather bound with paper perfect for ink and quill, as well as water colour. So, I bought a fancy pen and a paint pallet. I needed to remember. The vignettes here are from that book, the images faint reflections of bad water colours. "I lived in a house older than the United States." I loved that line. My mom visited and informed me that I had a problem with the back of the house. It slanted a little downward. I told her that was because it was nearly three hundred years old and part of the charm.

That leather book is really beautiful—handcrafted leather and handmade paper. It was a joy to handle it, write in it, paint in it. It now lives in a wooden box in which I keep little specials and memories. I call it 'The Grandkid's Box', because they'll get it when I'm gone. They can go through the contents, have a play or explore. Moving around the world discourages hoarding, so what's inside this box is the good stuff, like my grandfather's pocket watch, a dream journal, boxes of bits and pieces. Even a couple collections of poems. I tried to choose a few for this book that weren't terribly high on the cringe-o-meter.

There are also some short stories in these pages. There was a great Irish pub near my house in Canterbury. The city swells to double its size during the university term. Most of the pubs become rather unpleasant during that time (students, bleh!) but this Irish pub had a very subtle yet effective energy that seemed to repel the youngsters. I'd sit inside with a pint or three of Guinness and a yellow notepad and scribble away. The stories included here *were* actually written in that pub, but they have been reworked and rewritten since then, even published in journals or anthologies.

I have a story that doesn't quite fit anywhere, so will put it here. I met the character many times, and after combing out many of his children and brothers and sisters and their children, this story was born. I used to think headlice was something only the soldiers in the trenches of the First World War got, but I was educated properly once the girls started going to school. I made a game out of fighting the dreaded pests—I'd sit with one of my daughters, Number 1 or Number 2, with a bowl of soapy water each and a lice comb, and we'd see who could get the most. One afternoon Natasha, (Daughter Number 2) helped me finish this story. We pasted the text into a book and she illustrated it. Consider it an interlude in the introduction.

Interlude: Harry the Headlice, a story by Chris and Natasha

Well, come a little closer then! That's it! Closer still! Yeah! Put your head right up against mine!

There we go, now at least you can feel me even if you can't see me.

You see, I'm a very small little creature, and I'm very friendly. Whenever somebody gets close, I just pop over for a visit.

Sometimes, I even bring my family! I've got a big family and they'd all like to meet you!

I love to live in clean hairy places. That's where I find my food. I just get down to the ground and take a bite! I love the taste of fresh scalp! Yummy!

And those long clean hairs are just great for laying eggs on. Hundreds of eggs! Just stick them on, and they don't come off. They're so cute, I call them my little nits!

I gotta go and have a snack now. So, if you feel an itch, say 'hello', and we can have a chat as soon as I've eaten.

And yes, there were sequels. There was *Harry through History* ("Hallo everybody! Some say the dog is man's best friend, but really, I am—Harry the Headlice!"), *Harry on Holiday*, and *Harry gets Married*. The last two are unfortunately lost to us.

Interlude over. That isn't really the middle of this explanation-slash-introduction, it's more like the end. But before that, I do want to thank, from the depths of my heart, all those in the Isles that touched me and helped me become who I am.

Christopher McMaster
Wainui

On an Island Surrounded by Water

Reflections of the British Isles

Some scenes

Some scenes can easily be taken for granted—a river too timid or apathetic to finish its journey, daffodils already in the sorrow of old age below trees just beginning to yawn and welcome a spring that—gauging by cold fingers and grey skies—is still but a promise. With a sun blazing on the dry earth once I leave these islands will I wish to visit this place, to touch the damp soil and feel refreshed? How easy it is to overlook a seemingly common or familiar moment.

On a trip to Venice, I found a handmade note book—leather bound with paper perfect for ink and quill, as well as water color. So, I bought a fancy pen and a paint pallet. I needed to remember.

2 King Street

I lived in a house that was older than the United States. I thought that epitaph long before I moved out. The exercise was one of trying to bring back what it may have looked like fifty, one hundred, or one hundred and fifty years ago. The further back, the more skill and money needed. Still, I touched ghosts as I sanded old floorboards and door frames. The man who made this is long dead, I thought, as are any that may have remembered him. He lived, worked, loved (one hopes), dreamed (maybe), and this bit of wood may be all that is left of his time here. So, I sand with more care, more respect.

Zen and the art of wood stain.

Some nights I looked for memories, wisps of memories of those that slept or listened before. I know the wood is steeped in the sounds of the past, since I caught a glimpse (as you do) of the old man looking at the next tenant. Was he in the house when he died, alone in that lonely unkempt place, sitting in the old chair I found placed before the small fireplace? Was he pleased with my work?

Mostly they were silent, my housemates of long ago. The question I don't ask is: what ghosts will I leave behind? Perhaps (the main) reason that I will not miss this abode is the knowledge that I would not want to listen one night and hear them. Let them lie like leaves on the forest floor, to slowly wither and dry, to decompose and in turn nourish new growth, a new chance.

It is nice to think of this house's silence as being borne out of the past's respect for the present.

I will listen, one last time, before I close this green front door for the last time. I can already hear the quiet that will fill the rooms, the same quiet I heard when I opened it for the first time, only now with ears more appreciative to the spirits that remained silent.

The Miller's Arms, River Stout

Number 2 King Street, Canterbury, Kent

Highlands

The Highlands were the one place in the British Isles where I felt at home. I opened my lungs and breathed deeply for the first time, that first time I gazed at their desolate and cold peaks. I wanted to stop and feel them longer, to take them inside my very being, but the weather, or the light, or the kids, or the schedule conspired to prevent satisfaction.

I doubt that I will ever be satisfied. Not content with the view as a passenger, safe behind glass, I want to touch it. Not satisfied with a short break, a rest stop, I want to walk it. Still too low, I want to climb it. I want to hear it, to feel it, to watch its stars emerge at night to tell another story. A day, a week, a month—perhaps not yet in this life.

Then I realize it would not be enough until I became the mountains, until I became a moss-covered stone, a perch for bird and frost. It would not be enough until I disappeared among the mountains. Maybe, just maybe, that is where the feeling of home lies. No other place on this side of the world holds that for me.

There is a hint of dissatisfaction in life—of just being given enough to whet the appetite, but not enough to fill the soul. I am sure, on further reflection, that that sentence will be amended. The calm green hills of the south fill the hours, but it is the moments gazing at the vista that expands the mind and fills the heart, fills them with that clear, refreshing, cool stuff that is joy.

The Scottish Highlands in February

Cairngorm Mountains, Scotland

Skellig Rocks

We laughed when the boat tossed us and the sea filled our mouths and eyes. Eyes smiled across the small deck as the mainland receded—black, inhospitable cliffs. The crash of waves could still be heard over the straining engine, even above the smack of the bow as it rose and fell in the oncoming surf. Up and down like a ride at the funfair, white knuckles and all, as each of us held on. The sea-water stung with the rain. It wasn't clear which was the coldest.

Then the smiles slowly faded. Ten minutes slipped by. We began to realise, collectively and simultaneously, that our journey would last another hour and a half. We put on the rain gear proffered earlier and huddled for warmth. On first sight the rocks impressed a finality of sky and sea. Rising out of the grey and green they added black—sharp and stark, home only to the birds that add their own colouring, dirty white streaks of their, and countless of their ancestors', waste.

And yet, over a thousand years ago Irish monks inhabited one of these lonely rocks, climbing its rugged face to build a modest monastery out of the stones they found there. Their journey was by oar and certainly much longer and perilous than our pleasure cruise (compared to those faithful, and despite our drenching, what else could our fishing boat tour be called?) What greeted them—indeed, all they sought—was the cold and lonely place they found here. Shelter for the body—barely—but a refuge for the soul. Long days filled with prayer and meditation where only the sounds of nature, of sea and storm, of bird's cry would offer distraction. An idealised glance back, I admit, as I leave the soaked boat, soaked myself, back on the mainland and hastily retreating to the nearest coffee shop.

Skellig Rocks from a very wet tour boat

The Ring of Kerry, Ireland

Cliffs of Dover

Today a fog obscured the channel. The sound of ships calling to each other floats in the mist. On clear days you can see France and the beginning of the Pas du Calais. This is the closest you can get to the continent without a boat. From the opposite bank this green island must have looked an appealing conquest or refuge for ages of invaders and settlers. I 'discovered' this bay on my first days in England, having hours to wait for my ferry I picked a small squiggly line on the map that seemed to end at the sea itself. I followed the road and found that it did, indeed, stop there. I parked and sat for hours watching the waves lap at the shingle shore, the boats making their way through the twenty-mile channel, and the sun work its way as well, even lower than the ships, from one side of the channel to the other.

I had no idea that it would be the beginning of a very long stay.

Years later I returned seeking the same refuge I was offered before, and the tall white cliffs were still there, waiting like comforting arms to let me rest, to hold my worries and fears. The chalk of the cliff face crumbles over time, so they were, in some way, changed from my first visit. And, of course, I was changed as well.

That day I just let myself be held. There was nothing else to do, nowhere else to go. St. Margaret is the end of the road. There is nowhere else to run.

Such melodrama! In the following years I found myself living within fifteen miles of this place. I have walked the cliffs above, explored the shore below, even shown it to visiting family. But it is at its best when alone—then our past encounters blend with what passed in-between, mingled somehow with what will come to pass.

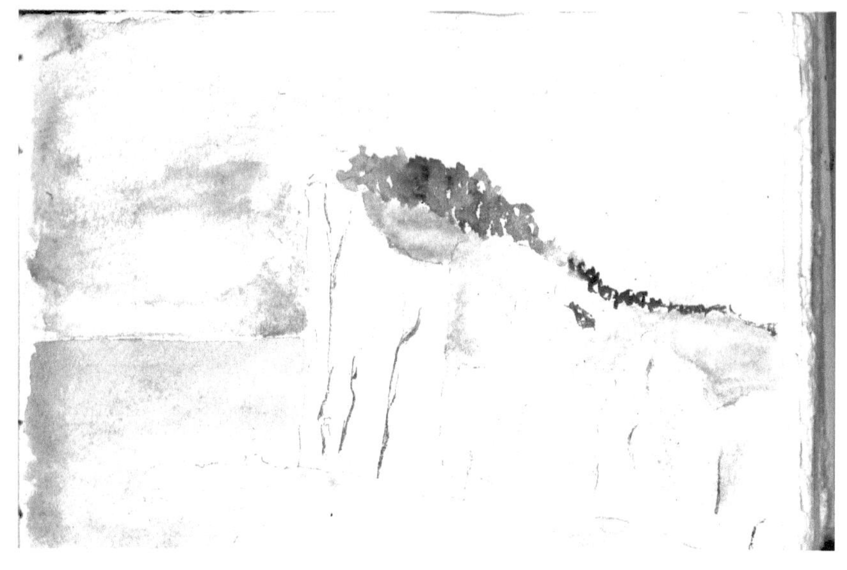

The Cliffs of Dover

St Margaret at Cliff, not too far above Dover

Dinghies in the Dover Harbour

Springtime

Springtime quietly sneaks up, like a timid young girl asking the boy to dance. By the time she is finished she will be an uninhibited temptress, seducing at will.

But summer is still far away.

The colour of winter is brown. Throw in some grey for wet, wet cloud, and of course some black—black for the night that begins so early and ends so late. Months seemingly increase in length; people begin to dress darkly reflecting their inner moods.

And there, like a gentle breeze, a soft breath against the back of the neck, and you begin to notice. The sun, though setting, is later. The lifeless branches that have continuously reached out to ensnare make the eyes refocus. They have somehow changed ...

Days pass—days now noticeably longer, noticeably lighter. The sinister trees of winter, seeming dead reminders of hope lost, are different. Though hard to see at first, there are buds! Hundreds and hundreds of buds on every strand. No longer painful reminders of a long-lost summer, they seem to quiver with a life furiously pent up, wanting to burst forth.

Rather than trudge from dark morn to cold eve, there is a collective skip, and as the fresh light green begins to fill the hillsides a restlessness fills the air.

"Would you like the dance?" she asks, so coy and innocent, while we all play along and say, "Yes! I thought you would never ask!"

Dane John Green, Canterbury, Kent

May in England

There are few places as beautiful as England in May. The entire countryside is awash with colour and life. The eye blurs and re-focuses, trying to ascertain if what is seen is real, or trying to simply take in all that shimmers before it.

Fields of rape glow yellow, their pungent odour filling the senses. New crops radiate green of all shades and offer games of guessing: what has the farmer decided to sow this season, in that healthy act of rotation? Standing in the woods there is a new calm—a near forgotten silence. The new leaves, twice, thrice, as large as last month act as sops to invading sounds. The road is no longer distinguished by swish of rubber. It is not heard at all.

Sitting motionless (and with patience!) can now be rewarded by the sight of that ever so bashful green woodpecker. My medicine animal, prying beneath the surface for sustenance. Or, if you are sitting upwind, a fleeting glance of the red fox—red orange blur in early evening hunt.

On a clear day the sky never darkens in its shade of blue. As it touches the horizon it lightens to a misty white, reminding continuously that this is indeed an island. The sky becomes the sea inverted—the blue of water confused as it reaches up and down, above and below. Now, looking at the distant hills (never really that far away, walkable before lunch) it is hard to be sure how green or how blue that landscape and sky really are.

When they are reached, they emerge just as bright and vibrant as those left behind. I am at play in my back garden, the one without the fence, the one that stretches from one coast to the other.

Elham Valley, Kent (The Garden of England')

Top Field, Barham Church of England Primary School

Community

A few days before Christmas, cold night but clear—rare diamonds sparkling above in a field of black. We are far enough from city or town to escape the orange hazy urban glow. We are far enough away to avoid the noise of too many people living too close together. Tonight, the air is filled with bells, calling the village to sit, to sing, where villagers have sat and sang for hundreds of years.

Walking up the hill I could feel alone, but it feels too nice in this moment by myself to wallow in selfish thoughts. I will soon sit with my children, who have practiced all week. I will walk by and smile at the bell ringers, who are also called friends. I will exchange pleasantries with parents, school governors, clerics.

Soon enough. The walk and the stars are a beautiful enough start.

And the church fills. Built by Norman hands, we sit among aged memories. After the service and after the singing we walk down the hill—this time as a community—to the school hall. There, mince pies and wines (red, white and mulled) await us. The children play, the adults chat, the teachers, after a long term, relax. We stop to watch a play—when did they rehearse that? —laugh and visit more. I try not to rush these experiences; they are worth being cherished. Foreigner, transient, visitor—these things I may be, indeed, these things I am guilty of feeling. But this night I am neither. I have a role. I am, after all, the village school teacher. I have a function and I am valued. I am part of a community.

This, in all honesty, is what I aspire to be. I am sure that I am not alone in that. The drive to position myself as such will guide most of my life, as it has so thus far. This experience, this night, is gentle instruction, nourishing taste.

So, like with a beautiful sunset, or a delicious cup of fresh coffee, or lovemaking by candlelight, I savour the moment, knowing it will soon enough end. I will chat in another corner, munch my pie, and let the wine fill my senses.

Barham Church, Kent, England

Barham School, hidden in trees

Grey

It is dry, but I haven't seen the sun for over a week. The sky is light grey, clouds that threaten boredom. It is a sky one accepts, even fails to notice. What becomes strange, leaving me feeling somewhat odd, is when the sky clears, when it is an empty blue with a warming bright orb suspended in it. In some ways it feels as if a heavy weight has been removed from my shoulders, that the ceiling has been lifted and I can stand upright.

In another way there is unease—this brief respite will be snatched away and the weight will be replaced! Nature unwittingly acts the tease, wakening brief memories of warm and clear days. She whispers, "Yes, yes, relax, let me touch you." And she does, for a while. But it is hard to surrender in this fickle clime. Learning to trust a summer that doesn't know its own mind. Maybe it is an impossible task.

But it is dry, and that should be appreciated. Buy a bike. Oil it well when not in use, and take advantage of days like this. There is a network of country lanes to explore, to watch pass by—the orchards, pastures, farms, woods, sleepy little villages with ancient churches and even older names. Listen in the quiet, a cacophony of life.

I may not trust the season, but I can celebrate it.

Rambling in the Rain

It was raining, but in a land where it usually does there comes a time when you have to stop caring. Keep the head and chest warm and dry, find a footpath, and walk. Rainy days are actually best because nobody else is fool enough to walk then, and the entire countryside is yours alone.

Bliss.

Freedom.

Public rights of way mean that if there is a fence, you can walk over it. If there is a farm, you can go through. As people have been using the footpaths for hundreds of years they have become as much a part of the landscape as a river or a forest or a cliff.

Choosing a direction. Easy—find the biggest road and walk the other way.

I was soon atop a small ridge with a village below. A few more minutes would put the church spire behind trees and an empty field turned to desolate and lonely landscape by the wet and grey sky. Face up, face down, it doesn't matter. What is in the mind of the solitary figure trudging across a sodden field? Imagination was left behind the last rise; worry and tedium dropped somewhere in the mud.

Right now, right here, there is nowhere else to be.

The map is a help, but used more for practice. It is impossible to get lost in the southeast. Mile after mile I become as empty as the landscape, which is the whole purpose of the exercise. The afternoon wears on and the increasing darkness becomes the only reason to head back. Past windows lit, cozy warm living rooms with families in front of televisions. Boy, did they miss out.

Bishopbourne, Kent

Memories

Which reminds me of the time:

We climbed that ancient oak in a Norfolk wood, naked as the day we were born, to watch the moon disappear behind our shadow.

And meditated for days in God's Thumbprint.

And talked to the stones and wind and anything else that would give me the time of day.

And driving the opposite way home to picnic beside Loch Ness.

And capsising in the harbor.

And waking to see a fox staring indignantly, pulling at my sleeping bag as if to say, "Piss off!"

And spiritualism, Hale-Bopp, and sewage thingies. Nobody will understand our code. But we can. Thanks for that.

Then there were the clouds racing past an orange sky with nobody to share them with.

Standing naked, arms outstretched under the season's first thunderstorm.

Being naughty in the park.

Finding four leaf clovers in the green.

That amazing evening in Jack's lounge in the faint light of the turf fire.

And getting mashed with Chris and playing the bongos all night long. Farafina!

And waking up on the river in Toad Hall.

Or lying back and watching the star filled Highland sky.

And bathing under a Lakeland waterfall after carrying those damn bikes to the top.

And hours with friends, the real jewels among this handful of gems, taken at random from the treasure chest of memories I will always hold dear—true souvenirs. The only ones of value.

River Thames, London, from the south bank

Humus

Sitting in this special place my fingers wander and work their way deeper into the earth, a lover's hand brushing and combing through hair. This cannot be removed, except by careful reflection. Sitting beneath trees, in soil that doesn't, directly, ever really see the sun, sitting on layer after layer of autumn harvest, those dazzling greens turned lifeless and brown, flying for a brief moment before coming to rest, right where I sit.

My fingers sink deeper, my toes can't resist and join in. This delicate layer is so rich, so cool, so refreshing. It is last year's beauty and pain, turned into new life. Breathing deep I imprint the smells, the feel, the feelings, and like a bag of this earth worn around my neck as a medallion, I close my eyes and take some with me, a shady and calm place hidden deep within.

Some Poems from Then

Etchings

Change swirls around me like a soft breeze through new green leaves and passersby look at my face raised and smiling wondering what there is to be happy about. "Can't you feel it?" I say, "Isn't it wonderful, just wonderful?" and they continue on bemused and confused and I raise my face smiling to that cool murmuring breeze once again.

Ah—gently, like your breath soft and warm against my cheek, there, there, a rhythm of its own, pulsing through hearts open and felt on faces raised and smiling and I say: "Why does my mouth taste of honey when I think of you?" but you don't pass by bemused or confused, answering me instead: "Isn't it wonderful, just wonderful?"

Thoughts of You

Go away
No! Don't go away
Stay and visit a while more
Walk with me as I go about my day
Sit with me while I rest and chat and read and work
Stay and visit a while more

Snapshots: Shamanic Journey

I see white. These are clouds.
There, clearing now, it is a meadow,
green and fresh with a river meandering
through it. There are people, dressed simply.
They seem happy, all of them.
They notice me and beckon.
I have heard of this place ...

No. I do know this place.
It is a picture people have painted
many times. It is just a picture, a concept, a limit.
To accept would be to limit.
Let it go. Let it go.

*

A lovely sound: swish, swish.
A nice combination, red lentil
and a touch of sand, put inside a dried gourd
to make a rattle. The ritual just clears the mind,
nothing more, just focuses the intention.

To the south, the west, the north, the east,

full circle completed.
Swish, swish, swish.

*

There is a story that shortly before his death
St. Augustine had an experience
of some sort, emerging from which only to say:
“All that I have said, all that I have thought or written,
is but straw.”
I’ve yet to find a source for this.
It has terrible ramifications
for a belief system. It’s also a great conversation piece
with any Jehovah's Witness.

*

Light again. A tunnel?
Light is a concept. A concept is a limitation.
Let it go. Let it go.

*

I am standing in a green setting
with a huge yellow sun in front.
Everything lifts so that I can see behind as well.
I am on a hand that lifts me up.
A mouth of stars breathes on me
and I tumble to earth. I hit the atmosphere
and burn bright, a falling star to any observer ...

*

Darkness, quite. There is no thought,
no expectation.
Just darkness. I am no more.
All ceases, there is only
the breath. In. Out. In. Out ...

*

"Let me explain, Donald.
It is like this: I am as much a part of you
as you are a part of you."

*

In. The breath. That is it.
I can stop the breath and enter fully into this,
stay here and my body
will not move again.
Out ... there—stop the breath—it is deeper.
In. Out ... joy, wholeness, love,
no word can enclose it. In.

The Sage

They have that tired look. Both of them. Dark rings under their eyes. They probably haven't had a decent night's sleep since she was born. Maybe a break or two. Maybe there is a capable grandparent. Or a children's unit offering respite. If so, I'll bet they don't take advantage of it too often. That smile. So full of love.

Her hand raises and is caught. Almost out of reflex. If unchecked she would catch her own hair and pull. There are many bald patches. And scars. I have only seen them at the family centre, but I am told that her room at home must have no sharp objects or edges. She wakes many times in the night threatening herself once again.

The image changes and sitting across the room is no longer a small child caught between heaven and earth whose brain was born damaged.

They must be learning so much about themselves.

Bathed in the Present

Remember that summer day
and thunder's clap opening heaven
we, standing upright
bathed in storm
clean and pure
heat and sweat washed away
with all past sins
standing there dripping
in blessed new moment
each moment
forgiving self its sins

City Break

I take my seat beside them
and am transformed
crowds pass indifferent
embarrassed or annoyed
"spare some loose change, sir?"
that wasn't from me
I don't wear the regulation
blanket and Alsatian pup
at this rate
in two hours time
they can buy it a tin of food
and eat it themselves
if they were serious

The Mountain

Standing quietly
Caught between heaven and earth
I find solitude

Bukowski is Still Dead

you've got some trajectory
you hit my neck
she said

i stole those lines
but i asked first
then she smeared it on my chest
and licked her fingers

bukowski is dead
and the *Rialto*
waxes poetic

she writes
with economy

each word
so dense
with memory
and meaning

like a kernel of popcorn

i want to fry her
in oil
and watch
her burst

damn
that would taste good

i want to
hang out
with my old friend
mr wolf
and eat shit
and howl at the moon

and bukowski is still dead

he can't even
eat popcorn
now

Alan

Ginsberg wanted to clean his ass
but his lover liked it dirty.

I saw him on TV and fell in love.
With what was coming out of his
mouth. And his soul. It's glow
filled the screen.

His exit was the best. Golden.
With friends and monks and film crews.

I want to die like that.

Snapshots: Bottoming Out

She'll come soon. I will hear the key first,
then the door closing. Too loud.
Always too loud at this time of night.
She'll be home soon. Liar.
My head spins. Why can't I control these thoughts?
This is unlike me. This is not like me.
How many hours have passed already?
How will I cope tomorrow,
bleary eyed and dopey?
She'll be home soon.
Yeah, but smelling of who?
She'll climb into bed trying to be quite
with that musky smell, lying miles away but mere inches.
Those terrible, terrible, lonely inches.
These thoughts race without me.
My stomach hurts. It must be time now.

*

Key sounds in door.
There are lights downstairs.
They are turned off and stairs creak.
The bedroom door opens and he lies

motionless pretending to sleep.

*

There in the bathroom is a bottle
of 800mg Ibuprofen. Pain killers.
That is what they are. They would help me sleep.
Such a new thought. Such a new place.
Nothing will ever be the same again.

*

The pattern on the sofa folds around me
while this music encases my soul
like some black fog. I cannot move,
my legs have no sensation,
my belly is full of sand, such an unbearable weight.
"It's okay babe, daddy is just upset."
Am I frightening her? Will she hug me or run away?
It is so lonely here. Where is my brave face?
"I'll be okay. Sometimes we all need to cry."
God, how much of this can she understand?
Draw the curtains. Turn off the lights.
I'll just sit here on my cushion
at the bottom of this pit so deep no light can even reach.
Such a new place.

*

I am below the cliffs now.
They rise white and glaring in the sun shine.

On an Island Surrounded by Water

I sit among large stones exposed by the tide.
There is a feeling of safety,
cliffs like arms embracing. I'm not sure
how I got here.
I think I slept in my car last night.
I can see it now, parked in a small gravel lot ...

Perception

I saw a big sky in England
splashed in crimson and blue
and the island flattened
into an expanse of possible
dreamscapes in technicolour
stratospheric humid air humming

Wind Chimes

I am the Buddha
of non-attachment

which comes easy
with all my forgotten
possessions boxed in cellars
or someone else's room
with my empty shelves
and the music
that could coax
me to smile
collecting only dust
abandoned in hasty retreat
before the advancing past
leaving goods and ghosts
to be used at some
future date
if I can remember where
I left them
to establish a new front line
adorn a new trench

("they'll be building trenches

for a thousand years")

and I'll sit near the fire
if there is one
and think of nothing in particular

A Few Stories Written in an Irish Pub

Earth Story

It was magnificent, Tara decided, using the only word she could find that was appropriate. It was the most magnificent thing she had ever seen. She gazed up at the rocket. Its smooth surface reflected the light of the moon, painting the hull with silver. She craned her neck to try and see the windows near the cone where the pilots sat and controlled the ship. The stairs leading inside were down, and the entry door open. She could have climbed up and went inside, to look around as they were invited, but that could wait. She would enter soon enough.

"It's not bad for shuttle," a voice said.

Tara jumped, startled and a little embarrassed by the squeal she let escape.

"Sorry, I didn't mean to scare you," the voice said.

"You didn't scare me," Tara snapped.

She peered in the direction of the voice and saw one of the Homeworlders. He looked about her age, but as her eyes adjusted, she saw the cadet insignia on his shoulders, meaning he was perhaps a bit younger. Tara shook her head disapprovingly. Dark blue sash with gold braiding, an image of his ship, embroidered shoulder epaulet with even more gold braiding. They liked their costumes, these people.

She recognised him from the reception. If she were honest with her emotions, she was awed by the crowd, overwhelmed even. She had never seen so many strangers before. Through great effort she managed to keep her mouth from hanging open as she studied their uniforms, how they held their drinks and ate their food, and as the night progressed, even how they danced. Only when one of them tried to entice her onto the floor did she find it all too much and fled to the comfort of the night outside.

"Well, I am," the boy/young man/cadet said. "Scared. I'm just stumbling around out here trying not to bump into anything with teeth. How can you stand this darkness?"

"There is light enough," Tara answered, hearing the condescension in her own voice. She took a deep breath and exhaled slowly. None of this was his fault, even if he made a fine target. It was churlish to lash out.

"The night at home is filled with light," he went on, ignoring or not noticing her rudeness. "The star cluster fills the entire sky, not like this dim splash of light. Darkness and pinpoints of light, looking into the disc from the edge of the galaxy. We're so far from home!"

"I am home," Tara said.

"Well, not for long," the cadet said. "I'm Sarn. I crew on the ship."

"I can see," Tara said. "The uniform gives it away. Cadet?"

"Cadet First Class," Sarn said defensively. "I ... I'm training to be an officer."

Tara felt her shoulders relax, as if a weight had been removed. She had been carrying a great deal, too much for a woman so young. She found her annoyance or anger at the Homeworlder not worth the effort, so on an unconscious level, set it down.

"I am Tara," she said, trying to be polite. The Homeworlder's ease made her self-conscious, feeling prim and old-fashioned, just like she felt ever since they arrived. "I am sure it must be very exciting," she added, looking up at the ship again and sounding prim and old-fashioned.

"You should have felt the thrusters coming down," he said. "She was really rocking as we burned through the atmosphere. But don't worry. It's always smoother going up, and we run a safe operation. And then you'll see the *Stellar Gem.* What a ship! Have you been topside?"

"Topside?"

"In orbit, above the planet, floating above it all."

"No," Tara answered.

"You're in for a treat then!" Sarn said, his excitement causing him to speak quickly. "She's an incredible planet. So much ocean, circling that huge continent. Beautiful green and blue, with white clouds swirling above it all. Oh, man," he added. "It's a shame she's going to be smashed."

Tara shifted her gaze away from the ship and towards Sarn. He was too young to read the subtle shift in her posture, and his eyes were unable in the faint light to see the corners of her mouth turn downwards. He ploughed on excitedly.

"That'd be something to see. An asteroid three kilometers across crashing into it. Bam!" he said, hitting his palm with a fist. "Dust clouds filling the sky, the crust so fractured volcanoes erupting everywhere, tidal waves hundreds of meters high! Acid rain. Acid fog. Imagine that! It's going to wipe everything out. The scientists on board want to stay and watch it. I mean, who wouldn't! But Captain won't stick around 'cause of the suicides. She says it'd be disrespectful, so we'll be well under way by the time it hits."

"What did you call them?" Tara asked.

"Call who?" Sarn asked.

"Those that are choosing to stay behind," Tara said slowly.

"Those that are ... oh, the *suicides*," Sarn said. "What else can you call them? We're here to evacuate you, to save you, and they want to stay, knowing what's going to happen—"

"Don't call them that!" Tara said, picking up her anger again.

"What, the suicides?" Sarn asked.

"I told you not to call them that!" she shouted.

Sarn watched as Tara stomped off into the dark jungle. He scratched behind his ear, furrowed his brow and tried to think of what he may have said that made her storm off. Captain said these people may act unpredictably, that the crew must show respect. She said they might be—how did she put it? *Traumatised?*

Shaking his head, he followed the sound of music and returned to the reception.

Tara looked out over the field, watching the cynodonts graze. She smiled at the sight of their squat bodies, remembering what she asked her grandmother when she was just a youngling. It had become a family joke.

"Why do they look like they're always about to take a poo?" young Tara asked.

She couldn't recall her grandmother's answer. And she still thought they looked like they were about to defecate. Strong front shoulders at the end of long front legs, short hind legs and fat haunches—that was where the best cuts were, her grandmother often pointed out. She dreamed of farming them for their meat, breeding them in captivity, selling the steaks to the colony, even exporting off world. Grandfather would roll his eyes at the old woman explaining the same plan, going over new problems and solutions that would eventually fail. But her dream survived her husband, and she found another to tell it to, her granddaughter. It was easier than talking about more important things.

"I'm pretty sure with the new frequency they'll stay put," she said as she poured tea. "Buggers just don't like to stay put, even with the beautiful grazing land I give 'em."

She was talking about the sonic fence again. But Tara didn't want to change the subject or tune her out like in the past. She felt ashamed that she had ever done that, and wanted this moment to never end.

"The sonic fence?" Tara asked.

"You bet," she smiled. "They got that large head, but it ain't filled with much. I tried again last week. They just stand there in the sound wave, can't seem to move out of it, just stand there until whatever brains they have starts to melt out their ears. Lost three that way until I could turn the damn fence off. Meat locker is full, anyway. Couldn't just let them go to waste."

Tara let her grandmother's words fill her. They had the same familiarity as the constant drone of insects, the soundtrack of her life, and of everything else she knew and took comfort from. And soon it would be gone. She bit her lip, glanced at her grandmother, retreated into her tea cup, took a sip, and searched for the courage to ask one more time.

But her grandmother got in first, delaying the inevitable. "I know, the grain has been a success. It's that what fed the colony, and made the family prosper. But I always wanted to be a rancher. There's a special kind of pleasure working with the animals, even if they are dumb brutes."

"Is that Betsa down there?" Tara asked.

She peered over the railing at the cynodont Tara pointed at. The creature turned and pointed her black eyes in their direction, as if knowing she was talked about. Tara watched as the beast chewed, trying to remember what her grandmother told her was so special about an animal on this planet being able to eat and breathe at the same time.

"Now that one just won't leave," her grandmother said. "Her eggs hatch and those little ones just wander away, but not her. She ain't going anywhere, who knows why."

"Why won't you come with us, Grandmother?" Tara asked, finally finding the courage to bring it up. Again.

"Oh, Sweetums, we've been over this already," she said slowly.

"But Grandmother," Tara pleaded, "none of this will survive. The farm, the ranch, the cynodonts. Nothing."

"You are young, and starting over is for the young," she answered. It was not the first time she made that statement, but this time it was with more compassion towards her granddaughter and the pain she was feeling. "Even your parents are still young enough to start over. But I'm not young. I buried my parents here, your great grandparents. And they are buried next to their parents. It is fitting I am buried next to them."

"Come with us," Tara said. "You do not have to start again. We will do that. You can retire!"

"Retire! Can you imagine that?" her grandmother chided. She placed a hand on her forearm, looking into Tara's eyes. "Honey, stop it," she said gently. "I am staying. I am okay with that."

"But I'm not okay with that." It came out as a whimper, and it was all she could do to stop herself from crying.

Her grandmother squeezed her arm. "Tara, you will take with you memories, where I will always be, and even though it hurts, you will also take a strong heart, a heart that knows about loss, and thus knows how to love." She smiled at her granddaughter and got up from the table.

"I have something else for you to take," she said. She walked to a tall cupboard and removed a polished wooden box. Bringing it back to the table, she set it in front of Tara.

"What's in this box belongs to the family," she said. "I gift them to you, to gift to your granddaughter." Tara knew the contents. The sash and the crest badge inside were worn by her great-great matriarch upon landing on this world. She placed her hands on the lid and had no more words to stop her tears.

Tara checked herself in the mirror, the future matriarch of her clan. She adjusted the sash on her shoulder, straightening the tartan cloth for the umpteenth time. She touched the family crest, pinned where the sash passed over her chest. She removed the lid of the jar containing the lotion her mother made from plants in their own garden, and gave to her for this occasion. She dipped two fingers into the jar and rubbed the lotion onto her arms, and then her hips and legs, taking her time despite time being limited.

When she was satisfied with the sheen of her scales, she joined her parents, and together they made their way to the waiting rocket.

The Bardo

Taan wrestled with the controls, but couldn't stop the spin. He had gotten too close, drawn by an unimaginable force, and his will was too weak. He wanted to see, to touch, to explore—every part of his being drawn to the blue green sphere. It vibrated with a force that was irresistible. He knew the risk, as well as the danger, but it wasn't enough to avoid the trap. The biosphere pulsed around the globe, the life contained within reaching out like solar flares, grasping and inviting, drawing down to the fertile planet below. And it reached out and grabbed Taan, who got too close because his will was too weak, and the planet was too strong.

As he fell, his view became a blur of black space and colourful planet, switching places too quickly. He tried to slow his spin, his descent, his fall, but over corrected. He felt his body shift with the inertia, pinning him to one side of the cockpit. His consciousness began to dim, a faint darkening in the corner of his vision. Fighting to maintain focus, he forced the controls, but the spin didn't slow. His world became white as his ship plummeted through cloud, and then the surface emerged. Colours flashed by, white, and green, and blue. The controls were useless, but he continued to pull on them. The clouds became more distant and the planet rose to meet him. Taan tried to keep his eyes open until the final moment, when his ship crashed in a blinding explosion on the surface.

Taan opened his eyes after days of darkness. He sought familiar warmth and wiggled with those around him, all competing for the nourishing liquid. There was enough for all. His mouth opened and closed until it latched onto the source. He was consumed with a hunger that was never sated, and he drank hungrily. Only when his small stomach was full and a sleepy contentment overwhelmed him did he think of the stars, of a distant home, of a ship spinning, of a name. *I have a name!* he thought, but sleep came and he forgot.

Over days he grew in size and strength. His eyes became sharp, at least for what lay close to his whiskers. His nose was sharper, guiding him to other scents, to seeds and crumbs and exciting opportunities. He explored farther, sometimes with his siblings, but more frequently alone. He kept to the shadows because danger lurked in the light. It lurked in the air above. It lurked around corners. Danger was everywhere, so he moved fast. He moved fast in his dreams, images that made less and less sense, clouds and greens and blues and danger. Taan twitched his nostrils and followed a delicious smell. He was drawn forward, as if the smell was reaching for him, grasping and inviting. *A beautiful planet!* Taan thought, though the words carried no meaning.

His eyes fixed on the prize that his nose had won for him. His mouth watered and his feet carried him towards the yellow cube. He opened his jaws and joyously bit into the prize and heard the snap of the trap that crushed his back.

Taan saw white and green and blue and white and green and blue and fire and dark and yellow and warmth and milk and then all was darkness.

Taan was trapped. His secure and comforting shelter was now claustrophobic. Suffocating. He had to get out! He pushed with weak feet and legs. His back was too fragile to wedge against the walls. So he swung his head forward, striking his prison with the middle of his face. He struck again, and again, only resting when his efforts were rewarded with a crack in his prison. There was a way out, a possibility of escape, of regaining control and returning home. He had to get home, and he was trapped. He pecked again, he used his frail body, and the walls around him began to crumble.

Taan emerged cold and naked and blind, but warm soft feathers soon surrounded him. He worked his head free and opened his mouth, an instinct, nothing more, and a hard beak stuffed food deep into his throat. He swallowed and named the sensation: hunger. His mouth opened again and again, demanding more, and more was given.

Over days, he grew. His naked skin began to be covered, and his eyes received light, slowly able to focus on his surroundings. Sometimes he was left alone, and he felt alone and far from home, even though he was home. During these times he opened his arms, arms that seemed light enough to hold the air. He knew, somehow, that one day they would, and he would fly. He knew he flew before, and he would again. Soon. He also knew he had a name, but he could not remember what it was.

But Taan never did fly. He was alone, again, his parents seeking food for his growing body, when he heard a rustle nearby. He made himself still and small, but he was hunted by smell, not movement or sight, and his scent was captured. As the approaching noise grew louder, he made himself as large as he could, spreading his weak wings and opening his beak wide, protesting as loudly as he could. It was a mere squawk, a pathetic effort, and it was quickly silenced when sharp teeth crushed the bones of his frail head.

Taan saw white and green and blue and white and green and blue and fire and dark and yellow and warmth and milk and food stuffed deep into him and then all was darkness.

Taan cried as jagged air streamed into his raw and unused lungs. Again, and again, the air scratched him inside. His eyes burned in the glare, even when closed as tightly as possible. All warmth escaped. He was naked and blinded and helpless. Taan cried more, and his lungs hurt worse. Finally, he was covered and moved and placed on a living bed of warmth, a warmth he knew because he shared it before, nestled and growing inside of it. He relaxed into a comforting familiarity, and opened his mouth, searching with lips, as if possessed by a spell. They closed and he suckled, filling his mouth, his throat, his belly, and he had no name or home other than this one, at this moment.

The Ethnographer's Gift

The man in the front of the car was angry, you could tell by the expression on his face. He was having trouble navigating through the dense traffic. He was late. He was thinking about trying to get there on time, that his wife would be angry, that he had a splitting headache. The children in the back seat weren't helping. They were shouting at each other. And at him.

"Give it back! That's my book!"

"I'm just looking at it!"

"Give it back! You always take my things without asking!"

"Ow! Dad, she hit me!"

"Both of you knock it off, I'm trying to drive!" Now the man was also shouting.

"Don't! You hurt me!" The man adjusted his rear-view mirror and could see hands flailing. He took one hand off the wheel and blindly reached back. He lifted it and slapped downward, catching one of his daughters on her knee. There was another "Ow!" from the back seat.

The man felt bad. He rarely, if ever, raised his hands to his girls. The car, in a situation like this, with all the pressure and all the risk, was one of those occasions. The stress of the drive was overpowering him. His mind was full of conflict, you could clearly see that in his expression. He wanted to be somewhere else. He was agitated. He was angry. He felt guilt for losing his temper.

The girls went quiet. Their anger at each other lingered. It sat between them like a sack of garbage polluting the back seat.

The father turned his head, just for a moment, to look at his girls. He saw them hurt, scowling, staring down at their knees. He wanted to see their eyes. To say, with a simple look, that he was sorry. He didn't see the truck travelling down a road on the right. The truck driver didn't see the red light. The sounds of metal meeting metal and the shattering of glass were deafening.

When the noise stopped the man and his daughters lay lifeless in the wreckage.

"Why are you showing me this?" Chloe asked. She was visibly upset by what she saw. She crossed her arms as if to give herself a reassuring hug.

"This is one of my favourites," she was answered. "Did you see the look on the girls' faces?"

"Yes, I did," Chloe said coldly. She didn't like what she watched. It worried and frightened her.

But her companion went on, sounding more excited. "They really loved each other very much. They were just like any family. They just got lost in the heat and the boredom."

"They're really dead now?" Chloe asked.

"Oh yes, they are," he answered. "I think they both knew they loved each other. Like the father. His expression, after he smacked his daughter, you saw that?"

"Yes. Yes, I did." Chloe, in fact, couldn't get it out of her mind. It was an angry look, but also soft and sad. His ...

"His last moment, what an amazing moment," Chloe's companion interrupted her thoughts.

"Here, take a look at this one," he continued. Chloe watched as he reached into a leather satchel and withdrew another glass-like ball. He could have lifted it with one hand but he used both with great care. He set it down on the table in front of her. It was opaque and smooth and round.

Chloe had just met this man. He spoke to her and sounded friendly. He seemed to have sensed her loneliness as she sat at the park table, hardly aware of others enjoying the fresh autumn sunshine. She wore her solitude like a comfortable coat, content to live more in what she had lost than where she was at the moment. Still, she found herself welcoming this stranger's intrusion. He was smiling as he approached, asked if he could join her. She found herself smiling in response and indicating to the empty bench. She couldn't quite remember his polite comments that broke the ice between them, but they somehow warmed her, somehow disarmed her.

Now she sat transfixed, gazing at the sphere the stranger had just placed on the table. She watched as the ball became clearer and shapes began to form.

The family woke in the middle of the night. Their subconscious, their dreaming selves, sensed something wasn't right. It couldn't identify what or why, but its cry was enough to wake them. The mother was first to realise what was amiss. She shook her husband roughly.

"Dan! Wake up! There's a fire in the house!"

Dan's eyes opened wide. He lay motionless for a moment until his sleeping mind joined his waking body. He saw the room was filled with smoke. His lungs hurt, his eyes watered.

"The kids!" he thought.

"Get up!" He shouted. "Get out of the house, I'll get the kids!"

He stumbled out of bed and rushed to the bedroom door. He put his hand against the wood to feel for heat before he slowly opened it. He found the hall full of smoke. It was very hot. There were flames below in the lounge. They would soon be climbing the stairs. He rushed to each of the three bedrooms, shouting into each room, "Get up, there's a fire! Get up! Come here!"

They would have to escape the house through the window at the end of the hall. His wife was already there. She had opened the window and was helping the first child, a boy of about six, through the window frame. It was a three metre drop to the ground, but it was the only way out. A second child, a girl, and slightly younger, came out and joined her mother. She was crying.

"Nick!" the father was shouting. "Nicolas!"

He turned to the girl. "Where is your brother Nick?" he demanded.

The girl looked at her father and continued to cry, speechless and too frightened to speak.

The fire was rapidly ascending to the first floor, drawn by the open window. The heat was becoming unbearable. Dan shouted again for Nick, but was answered only by the crackle of the fire. He shielded his face from the heat and entered a bedroom. His skin was blistering. He shouted again for his son, he tried to look in corners, to see through the heat and smoke, but had to retreat from the inferno. He ran, stumbling, coughing, down the hall, tripping and falling through the window.

Nick crouched trembling in the wardrobe. He couldn't see in the pitch-black darkness but his eyes were wide and scared. Every fibre in his being was trying to get away from the heat, the heat that grew worse every second. He tried to move to the left, then to the right. He pushed as deeply into the wardrobe as possible. He was screaming. He was crying. He was coughing, gasping for breath.

The heat grew so intense his hair crinkled and singed. Finally, in a moment of agony that felt like an eternity, he passed out.

“Perhaps I shouldn’t have shown you that one yet. It is very disturbing.”

Chloe was crying softly as the images in the glass ball faded.

“It is very powerful, a very intense moment. He suffered greatly.” The man Chloe had just met carefully took the glass ball and placed it back into his satchel. She heard it clack against others. Chloe looked at him now with a little fear in her eyes. She didn’t even know his name. She was sitting at the park picnic table, minding her own business, and yet she welcomed his company. Now she was worried about all this death and pain he was showing her in his magical glass spheres.

“Are they real, the people in the balls?” Chloe asked.

“They were once,” the man replied. “But what you watched were more like ... memories. Like snapshots of a moment.”

“Are they all the same type of moment?” Chloe meant of people dying. She was thinking all of this rather ghoulish.

“You mean of death, of the death moment. Yes, they are. It is very unique, very special.” He seemed pleased somebody was interested and apparently unaware of Chloe’s growing discomfort. An excitement was returning to his voice.

“Who are you?” Chloe asked.

“I am a researcher. I do field research. I study people. You might call me an anthropologist, or an ethnographer.”

A small shiver ran through Chloe as she looked more closely at the man sitting across from her. She wanted to ask her question again. She searched for words to rephrase it. “You are not from here, are you?” she finally said.

"No, I am not," he answered slowly. He looked into the blue sky. "Were it dark now, I could perhaps point to a distant light." Then he remained silent.

He was forcing her to search for more words. There was a game of sorts going on now. He seemed to want to tell her something more. She wanted to know what it was, but didn't know how to ask.

"Why do you collect these moments?" she tried.

"What a wonderful question," he smiled. "These moments, they are so unique. It is the time when what you might call the spirit separates from the body, when the life that fills you leaves."

"But everything dies, what is so unique about that?"

"Where I come from it doesn't happen in quite the same way. Not the same way at all. And when a life is to leave, I am there, as if by instinct. My collections are actually very well known among my kind. What did you notice about each of the people in what I showed you?"

Chloe thought for a moment. "They didn't expect it or want it to happen,' she said.

"Exactly! In every life there is a moment, only one moment, when that life will leave its physical form. And in moment after moment, satchel after satchel, there is fear, regret, pain ..." his voice trailed off. It seemed tinged with sadness.

Chloe interrupted the silence that settled between them. "It sounds so terrible, so awful."

"Yes, it is. Sometimes terribly sad. My study is really of the mind, and what fills the mind in its last conscious moments. It is such an important moment, one that is inevitable, but feared. So many people know that they will die, and yet they refuse to face it. And when it happens, they are totally unprepared. Nobody thinks that *today* they might die, only it is always a *today* that they do."

Chloe was watching, listening.

"This time," the stranger went on, "it is my objective to collect a moment where the individual is aware that it is their death moment. No pain, or fear, or suffering, but acceptance."

As he finished speaking Chloe slowly got up from her seat. "I really must be going now," she said.

He smiled at her and replied softly, "it was a pleasure meeting you."

As Chloe walked away, she noticed, for the first time, other people at the park. Children were playing. The wind was blowing coloured leaves through the air. She thought of glass balls, of strangers, of pain and suffering. She thought of her own pain, of love lost. She travelled back in memory to cosy mornings in bed, the smell of her lover's hair, the feel of his body beside her. She felt her muscles relax, her body warm. *I might die today*, she thought, and found herself smiling for the first time in months.

She wasn't paying attention as she stepped into the street, but the driver of the car would never forget the look on her face before he ran into her. Looking into the eyes of the driver, in the moment before impact, Chloe turned her head and saw her death. Her expression was one of peace, almost of happiness.

Books I've Written That You Should Read

American Dreamer

Lucid Book 1: *Can one person change a reality?*

Chicago. 1944. Waking in a dream Nadia finds herself in a class with two other students. The woman posing as their teacher, (if indeed she is a woman), convinces them that they have no real choice but to assist with her plan. Miss Biel breaks each of them with terrifying nightmares, and 'tasks' to complete while awake that destroys any hope of escape.

But Nadia begins to realize she isn't quite alone, not exactly powerless, and that there are those besides Miss Biel who want a certain outcome. There comes a time when she has to decide who to trust.

American Dreamer weaves present and past in a narrative that transports the reader to an earlier age, and slowly wakes them to an alternative reality, not too distant than our own present.

"A great story, imaginative and absorbing. I read the whole book over a weekend, couldn't put it down. The crossing between alternate universes and parallel lives was like American Gods written by Neil Gaiman. It was a reminder that even in these troubled times, things could be worse!"

—Amazon reviewer

Tomorrow's History

Lucid Book 2: *Can one person save a reality?*

London. Present day. Sunlight glints off solar panels, harvesting the energy that keeps the city moving. Roof gardens add a hint of green to the skyline. Airships pass overhead on their way north to the capital, Jorvik. Ships of the Great Fleet load at the busy docks, preparing for the voyage across the Western Ocean to the Far Settlements, holding the Norse world together.

Jakob thinks his world is safe. But it isn't. Something needs finishing for his present to come to pass, and for some unknown reason he has been chosen to do it. Trapped in his dreams, and thrust into an age of Vikings who are much more familiar with the sword and the axe, he uses the only thing he has—his wits.

Tasked with leading a party of Danes in pursuit of royal game, he is swept into an adventure that can only have one outcome if Britain, and the Danelaw, is to survive.

Tomorrow's History has it all. Gods and goddesses, Vikings, time travel, alternate realities, lucid dreams ... and key moments in history, where the very future hinges on the outcome.

Gods and Dreamers

Lucid Book 3: *Time kills all things. Even the gods.*

We all dream. Only most of don't remember. How can we even know what we do in our dreams if the memory fades like mist when we wake? Teeny, Robbie, and Thieu start to recall their dreams and the disturbing acts of violence and servitude that they are coerced into committing in timelines other than theirs.

Awareness breeds rebellion. Led by Petrit and Nadia, who enlist the new rebels into their secret campaign against the manipulative gods, the dreamers learn how to use their lucidity to resist the oppressive forces that control both their dreams and realities.

But first they have to survive. There are others who think them heretics and will try to stop them at all costs.

MisStep

Science fiction:

Stepping: The easiest way to get from point A to point B is to put A and B in the same place. Simply Step from one to the other. Known as an Einstein-Rosen bridge, it is theoretically possible. It just requires an immense amount of energy. And in a future where that energy is harnessed, that's what we do.

Jens needed to get off the planet in a hurry so he took the first job on an interstellar freighter he found—part of a convoy to a far-flung mining colony, three Steps and almost three thousand lightyears away. Only the desperate went so far—colonists willing to trade a life on Earth for a new start on a rock somewhere across the galaxy, or spacers one step ahead of the law.

But as each Step takes him farther from home, Jens learns that the job isn't exactly what he was told, the cargo not as legitimate, and his situation even more precarious. Jens finds himself being groomed for a role in an interplanetary drug racket, with no way out.

Then the convoy mis-Steps, emerging lightyears off course, and the miscalculation might not be their fault!

Seeders

The story continues—the exciting sequel to *MisStep:*

They tried to hide from certain death. Now it's time to find them.

A pandemic spread over their planet and swept them from history. In a desperate act to save their species they launched a remnant of survivors into the depths of space, frozen in cryo-sleep, to be awakened only when their ship detected a habitable planet. But there were no planets and the ship continued into the cold and dark.

Thousands of years later humans have settled the ocean world. Earth's dream of finding her sister planet has come true, and it was free for the taking. They gave it their own name, *Pemako*, and lived beside the ruins of what was once a mighty civilization. Picking through the artifacts, xeno-linquist Peter Taylor and a small research team find evidence of the Original's desperate mission. Plotting the probable course of the ship, the team locate where it might be, if it really exists, and if it is still operational.

The promised technology of the Originals outweighs any 'ifs'. But they need the help of a powerful earth-based consortia, as well as from Andrew Jensen, the only man to survive a confrontation with those whose planet they now call their own.

Pirates Come Down

Climate fiction meets science fiction in this high-seas adventure.

Fishing in the near future takes more than a net!

Rickets is a PAC-Man, his patrol and attack craft the first line of defense against encroaching vessels. Moss is a Fisheries Observer, tasked with ensuring companies abide by the quotas set on target species. Together they play a part in ensuring the waters are not fished to extinction.

But as fisheries elsewhere play out, New Zealand waters start to look more attractive until every ship protects itself with PAC boats, missiles that skim the surface, and kamikaze drones equipped with explosives.

Only there is a bigger shadow on the horizon, one that defects all radar, is lethally armed, and takes what it wants!

To learn more about Christopher's books, visit him at:

www.christophermcmaster.com

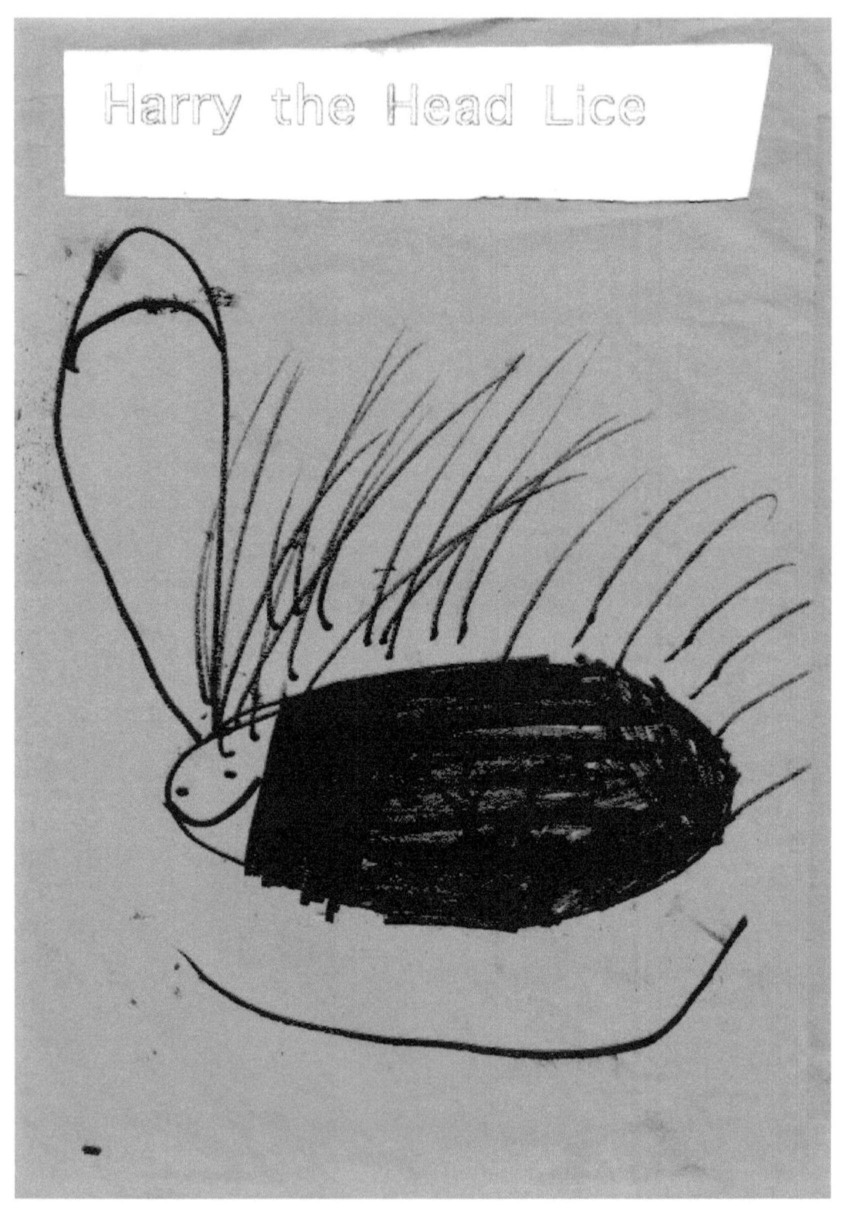
Harry the Head Lice

On an Island Surrounded by Water

www.ingramcontent.com/pod-product-compliance
Ingram Content Group UK Ltd.
Pitfield, Milton Keynes, MK11 3LW, UK
UKHW042013190726
13854UKWH00005B/2275

9 780473 589882